GREAT OUTDOORS
SPORTS ZONE

UPLAND BIRD

HUNTING WILD TURKEY, PHEASANT, GROUSE, QUAIL, AND MORE

Tom Carpenter

Lerner Publications Company • Minneapolis

Lerner Publications Company
A division of Lerner Publishing Group, Inc.
241 First Avenue North
Minneapolis, MN 55401 U.S.A.

Website address: www.lernerbooks.com

Content Consultant: James G. Dickson, PhD, wildlife biologist, researcher, author, professor,
and hunter

Library of Congress Cataloging-in-Publication Data

Carpenter, Tom, 1962–
　　　Upland bird hunting : wild turkey, pheasant, grouse, quail, and more / by Tom Carpenter.
　　　　　p.　cm.
　　　Includes index.
　　　ISBN 978-1-4677-0223-2 (lib. bdg. : alk. paper)
　　　1. Upland game bird shooting.　I. Title.
　SK323.C37　2013
　799.2′4—dc23　　　　　　　　　　　　　　　　　　　　　2012012214

Manufactured in the United States of America
1 – CG – 7/15/12

The images in this book are used with the permission of: Backgrounds: © Jason Lugo/iStockphoto; © Patrimonio
Designs Limited/Shutterstock Images; © Sabri Deniz Kizil/Shutterstock Images; © uspenskaya/Shutterstock
Images; © Linn Currie/Shutterstock Images, p. 4; © NanoStock/Shutterstock Images, p. 5; © Fred Lynch/AP
Images, p. 6; © Library of Congress, p. 7 (top, HABS MD,22-SHARP.V,19-A—1); © Pictureguy/Shutterstock Images,
p. 7 (bottom); © North Wind Picture Archives, p. 8; © Images in the Wild/iStockphoto, p. 9; © Tyler Olson/
Shutterstock Images, p. 10; © LaVonda Walton/USFWS, p. 11 (top); © Dave Menke/USFWS, pp. 11 (bottom),
24 (top); © Tony Campbell/Shutterstock Images, p. 12 (top); © Bruce MacQueen/Shutterstock Images, p. 12
(bottom); © George Gentry/USFWS, p. 13; © kali9/iStockphoto, p. 14; © Red Line Editorial, pp. 15, 23 (top),
29 (top); © Judy Kennamer/Shutterstock Images, p. 16; © Katherine Moffitt/iStockphoto, p. 17 (top); © Richard
Semik/Shutterstock Images, p. 17 (bottom); © Dan Bannister/Shutterstock Images, p. 18 (top); © Risteski Goce/
Shutterstock Images, p. 18 (bottom); © Dennis Hoyne/iStockphoto, p. 19; © F.C.G./Shutterstock, p. 20 (top); ©
Eric Isselée/Shutterstock, p. 20 (bottom); © Barna Tanko/Shutterstock Images, p. 21; © Brett Billings/USFWS , p.
22; © Lugo/iStockphoto, p. 23 (bottom); © Mark Duffy/Bigstock, p. 24 (middle); © Bryan Eastham/Shutterstock
Images, p. 24 (bottom); © Al Parker Photography/Shutterstock Images, p. 25 (top); © Andy Gehrig/iStockphoto,
p. 25 (middle); © USFWS, p. 25 (bottom); © Dewayne Flowers/Shutterstock Images, p. 26 (top); © James G.
Dickson, p. 26 (bottom); © Robert Burton/USFWS, p. 27; © Mshev/Shutterstock Images, p. 29 (bottom).
Front cover: © Peter Beck/CORBIS

Main body text set in Avenir LT Std 65 Medium 11/17.
Typeface provided by Adobe Systems.

TABLE OF CONTENTS

CHAPTER ONE

WHY HUNT UPLAND BIRDS?

Every fall, an exciting sport lures hunters to the places where upland birds live. Upland bird hunting takes place all across North America. Pheasants live in farmland and grasslands. Ruffed grouse dwell in young forests. Different species of quail call farms, deserts, or mountains home. Sharp-tailed grouse live in shortgrass prairies. Wild turkeys thrive almost everywhere. And there are many other kinds of upland birds to hunt too.

Hunting upland birds means getting exercise in the fresh air. You will explore beautiful countryside from endless prairies to colorful fall forests. Upland bird hunting is a great way to spend time with an older friend or family member. It is also a great way to spend time with a good bird dog. Upland birds are worth the challenge to bag (shoot and collect). Their meat tastes delicious.

A dog can help you in your upland bird hunt.

Upland bird hunting is a great way to spend time outside.

5

CHAPTER TWO

HISTORY OF UPLAND BIRD HUNTING

Native Americans were the first people in North America to hunt upland birds for food. Quail and grouse were common targets. So were wild turkeys.

Native Americans often used bows and arrows to hunt upland birds. Some hunters used a dart thrower called an atlatl. The trick was sneaking close enough to a bird to throw the atlatl. If the bird sensed the hunter coming, it would fly away before the hunter could throw the dart. These early hunters also used nets and baited traps to catch upland birds.

European Settlers

European settlers started arriving in North America in the 1500s. As settlers spread out across the continent,

A boy uses an atlatl. Though atlatls are ancient Native American hunting tools, atlatl competitions are still held in modern times.

Settlers cleared land to create small farms, like this one in Maryland.

things began to change for upland bird populations. The settlers cleared wooded land to create space for small farms. The newly opened space helped some upland bird populations grow. Prairie chickens were numerous before settlement, but numbers exploded as small grain farms popped up all over the landscape. Bobwhite quail numbers also increased. In the late 1800s, ring-necked pheasants were introduced from Asia and Europe. These birds flourished across much of North America.

Native Americans hunted prairie birds, such as grouse.

7

Settlers relied on upland birds for food in the early 1800s. By the late 1800s, upland birds had been overhunted.

Prairie chickens had almost been wiped out by the mid-1900s. They have made a comeback and can now be hunted in some places.

But the changes weren't all good. Eventually, big farms took the place of small fields. Bobwhite quail numbers began to drop. As more and more prairie grass was plowed to create big fields, prairie chicken populations took a dive.

Market hunting (hunting birds to sell to a market in town) began putting upland bird populations in even greater danger. Market hunters shipped prairie chickens from Minnesota and South Dakota to Chicago and East Coast markets in the late 1800s and the early 1900s. By the 1930s, prairie chickens were almost extinct (completely killed off).

With habitats (living spaces) reduced and no hunting regulations, upland bird populations were losing ground fast. Conservation (the smart use of natural resources) was born. In modern times, hunters are the chief conservationists for upland birds and their habitats.

CHAPTER THREE

PROTECTING UPLAND BIRDS

Protecting upland birds means protecting their habitats. A habitat includes where the bird finds shelter and food and raises its young. Different upland birds need different habitats. Sharp-tailed grouse need a low-grass habitat on the Great Plains or in the open land of the West. Ruffed grouse like young forest with lots of brush (low trees and bushes). Pheasants thrive in a mixed landscape of grainfields, grasslands, wetlands, pastures, and brushy areas. Wild turkeys can live almost anywhere trees and grass grow.

Big farms across North America have reduced upland bird habitats. But farmers also use their unplanted land to help bird populations to thrive.

A worker from the U.S. Fish and Wildlife Service teaches students how to plant wetland plants. Protecting upland bird habitats is important to the birds' survival.

What people do to the landscape can hurt or help upland birds. The Conservation Reserve Program (CRP) pays farmers to manage their fields in ways that help the environment. This includes turning poor cropland into grassland. New grassland means new habitats for pheasants, sharp-tails, and quail. Bobwhite quail do best where farmers' small grainfields of oats and rye mix with low grass and bushes.

Bobwhite quail like areas with low grass.

Hunting Seasons and Bag Limits

Biologists are scientists who study living things. They work with state fish and game agencies to set hunting seasons and bag limits. (Bag limits are rules about how many birds of a species (kind) a hunter can shoot in a day.) These rules help protect upland bird populations. Except for wild turkeys, most upland bird hunting seasons take place in the fall and winter. Upland birds do not migrate. They live in the same area year-round.

Conservation Organizations

Many conservation organizations exist to help protect upland birds. These organizations focus their efforts on preserving habitats. These groups include Pheasants Forever, Quail Forever, National Wild Turkey Federation, and Ruffed Grouse Society. Many members of these organizations are upland bird hunters.

Many organizations help preserve the habitats of upland birds, such as wild turkeys.

Officers from fish and game agencies help enforce the rules that protect upland birds.

CHAPTER FOUR

HUNTING SAFELY

A ny kind of hunting is a big responsibility. You must look out for your safety and for the safety of other people, hunting dogs, and property. Firearms safety is very important. You must buy a hunting license. It is your responsibility to get permission to hunt on private land and to know the boundaries of public land. You must follow all hunting rules and regulations. You must hunt in a way that's fair and considerate to the animal.

Safety Training

Most states require young hunters to take firearms or hunting safety courses. Not only is this the law, but it is also a smart idea.

Before you hit the hunting grounds, make sure you know all the rules to hunt responsibly.

FIREARMS SAFETY

Here is the basic formula for gun safety. Remember these letters: TAB-K.

- Treat every firearm as if it were loaded.
- Always point the muzzle (tip of the gun) in a safe direction.
- Be sure of your target and what lies beyond.
- Keep on the safety (a device that prevents accidental firing), and keep your finger off the trigger until you are ready to fire.

In a safety course, you will learn techniques for hunting safely so that you don't shoot or injure yourself or a fellow hunter.

SHOOTING ALLEYS

Shooting Alley 1

Shooting Alley 2

Shooting Alley 3

When hunting upland game, you're often walking near your hunting partners. It is important to identify and stay within your shooting alley (the area within which you are limited to shooting). This keeps you from accidentally shooting your partners.

WILDLIFE REFUGE

NO
Hunting, Trapping, Guns, Bows, Traps or Dogs Without Valid Permit

Where to Hunt

State game agencies list public hunting lands on their websites. If you're not sure the land is public, don't hunt there. Wildlife management areas and state and national land may offer good hunting. Make sure hunting is allowed before you go hunting on public land.

There is often good upland game hunting on private land. As a hunter, you are responsible for getting permission to hunt on private land. Be courteous when you ask to hunt. Show the landowner you are a responsible hunter. And thank the landowner after your hunt. That way, the spot could be yours to use in the future.

Know the rules where you are hunting. If a special hunting permit is required on public land, make sure you have it.

Hunting Regulations

When hunting, it's necessary to follow all regulations. Not knowing a law is not an excuse to break it. You can get regulations booklets at sporting goods stores, state offices, or on your state's fish and game agency website.

Some key regulations to know include the following:

Hunting season dates: Make sure hunting season is open.

Shooting times: Good light is needed when shooting. Find out when it is legal to shoot in the morning and how late you can shoot in the evening.

Bag limits: Different species of upland birds have different limits for how many birds you can harvest in a day.

Fair Chase

Good hunters follow a code of ethics beyond what's in a regulations booklet. Ethics means doing the right thing, even when no one else is watching. It means hunting in a way that is fair to animals and other hunters.

Good ethics include hunting with fair chase methods. For instance, many hunters think it's unfair to shoot an upland bird on the ground. Shooting a bird on the ground can also be dangerous to hunting dogs and other hunters. Work hard to find birds you have shot. A hunting dog can be a big help in finding downed game. Make the most of your game meat.

A well-trained dog will help you find the bird you shot.

CHAPTER FIVE

LET'S GO HUNTING!

It's almost time to go hunting! You don't need a lot of equipment to successfully hunt upland birds. But you do need the right gear. You also need to know the right hunting strategies.

Shotgun

A lightweight shotgun that is easy to carry is perfect for hunting upland birds. A 20-gauge shotgun is about right for young hunters. More experienced hunters may use the larger 12-gauge. Both shotguns are loaded with a shell. The shell includes a case that holds powder and shot pellets. When a hunter fires the shell, the pellets spread out and hit the game.

Clothes

Upland bird hunters wear lightweight, sturdy clothes that are comfortable to walk in but protect their skin from burrs and thorns. Because you are often hunting in the fall, temperatures can vary a lot. Dress in layers

Shotgun shell

12-gauge shotgun

BLAZE ORANGE IS A MUST

Always wear blaze-orange clothing when hunting upland birds (other than wild turkeys). Wear a blaze-orange hat, and make sure your hunting vest or coat has a lot of this bright, neon color. There is no color like blaze orange in nature. It makes you highly visible to other hunters. Blaze orange helps prevent shooting accidents.

so you can remove or add clothes when the temperature changes.

Outerwear

Wear a hunting jacket or vest with plenty of blaze orange. Your jacket or vest should have a game pouch (large pocket) in back to carry game you shoot. Other pockets will hold gear, and loops will hold shotgun shells. Wear a blaze-orange cap so other hunters can easily spot you.

Boots

Wear sturdy boots that are comfortable to walk in. Pheasant and grouse hunting may take you in or around wet areas, so waterproof boots are a good idea. Know what type of land you will be hunting on when picking your boots.

Accessories

Make sure you carry water for yourself and for your dog. You should have a bag or a strap to carry your game. Have a knife and game shears (a type of scissors) to clean your bird.

A blaze-orange vest, like the one this woman is wearing, will help you stand out from nature.

Upland Hunting Dogs

One of the upland bird hunter's greatest rewards is hunting with a bird dog. A good dog can help you find birds and then retrieve them after you make your shot. Training a good bird dog is challenging but rewarding work. There are two basic types of bird dogs: flushers and pointers.

Flushing Dogs

Flushing dogs work within your gun range as you walk. Their job is to locate birds, chase them, and get them to flush (fly away quickly) within the shooting range. If you make the shot, the dog finds the bird and brings it back to you. Excellent flushing dog breeds include the Labrador retriever, the golden retriever, the English springer spaniel, and the Boykin spaniel.

Pointing Dogs

Pointing dogs range (walk out) a little farther from you than

English springer spaniel

A hunting dog points at game in the grass.

flushing dogs. A pointing dog smells and finds the bird, then stops and points to it. To point, the dog stands perfectly rigid with its nose toward the bird. Birds will freeze when they see this. Then you can walk up and flush the bird and take your shot. Pointing dogs will often retrieve your bird too. Good pointing dog breeds include the Brittany spaniel, the English setter, the German shorthair pointer, and the English pointer.

DOG HUNTING TIPS

- Hunt into or across the wind so your dog can pick up bird scent.
- Don't try to outthink your dog. Hunting dogs have the natural ability to smell and find upland birds. Trust them.
- Look out for your dog. Carry a couple of water bottles, and give your dog drinks often. And don't let your dog get too hot or tired.

Walking quietly through upland habitats gives you a chance to flush the birds. Stay alert!

Upland Hunting Strategies

Early to midmorning and late afternoon are the best times for hunting upland birds. This is when they are looking for food. Because they are so active, they will leave a scent for your dog to find. During the middle of the day, most upland birds hide in thick cover.

Find out what habitat the species of bird you are hunting lives in. To hunt the bird, walk slowly through its habitat. Zigzag back and forth to cover more ground and confuse any birds hiding nearby. Stay alert and pause often. This makes the birds nervous. They may flush. If they do flush, you will be ready. Keep your gun ready to shoot at all times, but keep safety in mind.

Making the Shot

A bird flushes! Now what? Upland birds are challenging to hit in flight. Most hunters shoot over the bird or behind it. Here's how to shoot well:

Blocker   **Blocker**   **Blocker**

Pusher   **Pusher**   **Pusher**

Pheasant hunters often hunt in groups. In a group of six hunters, three hunters, called pushers, line up in a row with their dogs. This line walks into the wind through the pheasants' habitat. The other three hunters, called blockers, stand at the other end of the habitat. With this strategy, either the blockers or the pushers may get shots. Blockers and pushers must never shoot at each other.

Get your cheek down on the stock (back of the shotgun) when you shoot, and look right down the barrel.

Swing your shotgun past the bird, and pull the trigger as your gun's muzzle passes the bird. You will build a natural lead on the bird and avoid overshooting.

Most important, be safe. Always know where your hunting partners and your dogs are.

When an upland bird flushes, it's time to take your shot!

UPLAND BIRD GUIDE

RING-NECKED PHEASANT

Ring-necks prefer a mixed habitat of grasslands, grainfields, pastures, wetlands, and areas of low shrubs and trees. An average ring-neck weighs 2 to 3 pounds (0.9 to 1.3 kilograms). Listen for the male's *kyik-kuk kyik-kuk kiyik-kuk* cackle when he flushes. Don't let the long tail fool you—swing ahead for your shot.

BOBWHITE QUAIL

Bobwhite quail live in the farmland, grassland, and brushland of the eastern United States and the Great Plains. Quail do best in a mix of small fields or grassy meadows. Bobwhites are small. An adult weighs only about 8 ounces (226 grams). Follow a single bird after a covey (group of birds) flushes.

SHARP-TAILED GROUSE

Sharp-tails live in the wide-open grasslands and ranchlands of the Great Plains and the West. These grouse prefer short grass where they can easily see danger coming. Most sharp-tails weigh about 2 pounds (0.9 kg). You have to walk a long way for sharp-tails. Hunt in fields of short grass.

Ruffed grouse inhabit young woodlands where the trees are thick with lots of brush. A grouse usually weighs 1 to 2 pounds (0.5 to 0.9 kg). Grouse are hard to hit. You need to shoot fast, but be safe.

HUNGARIAN PARTRIDGE

Native to Europe, the Hungarian partridge has been in North America since the late 1800s. These birds prefer the grasslands of the northern United States and Canada. An average Hungarian partridge weighs only about 1 pound (0.5 kg). Walk through short grass trying to get a group of birds to flush. Then pick one bird to shoot.

PRAIRIE CHICKENS

Though endangered in some places, prairie chickens can still be hunted in some states, such as South Dakota and Kansas. An adult prairie chicken weights about 2 pounds (0.9 kg). Walk through tall grassland, and use a dog to help you find and flush prairie chickens.

HUNTING WILD TURKEYS

Wild turkey hunting is different from hunting other upland birds. Instead of wearing blaze orange, turkey hunters wear camouflage (fabric designed to blend in with nature) from head to toe. They do this because turkeys have very sharp eyesight. As a result, you need to always be aware of your surroundings and other hunters when turkey hunting.

You must stay as still as possible to keep a turkey from spotting you.

Spring Hunting

In spring, you can only shoot gobblers and jakes (male birds). Gobblers are adult turkeys, and jakes are less than two years old. Find an area with signs of turkeys. Set up with your back against a tree and your shotgun propped up on your knees. Sit very still. A turkey can spot even the smallest movement.

Spring is mating season. Gobblers will be out looking for a hen (female turkey). Use a turkey call to make the sounds of hens to attract a gobbler. If your hen noises sound real enough,

Turkey hunting is a fun and exciting sport.

Turkey hunting often takes place in the spring during mating season.

you may be able to lure a gobbler. When he gets in close enough, take your shot.

Fall Hunting

Fall turkey hunting of both gobblers and hens is allowed in some states. Turkeys flock (group together) during this time of year. Sneak up on a flock with your gun unloaded. Then rush in, yelling and whooping to startle the birds. Hopefully, the birds will fly in multiple directions. Then load your gun and set up with your back against a tree near the spot where the birds were gathered. Use hen or young turkey calls to lure the birds back into range. The scattered turkeys will want to return to the flock. Some birds may come running.

TURKEY CALLS

There are many different types of turkey calls. Some are created with mouth-operated instruments. Others involve the hunter running a wooden paddle or striker along a surface made of wood, aluminum, or another material. Pushpin calls are the easiest to use. The hunter presses a button or a pin to make the turkey sound. Whatever type of call you're using, the more you practice, the more you will sound like a real turkey.

UPLAND BIRD CARE, CLEANING, AND COOKING

Your upland hunt isn't over until you eat the game birds you shoot. To get a great meal, you need to know how to care for your birds in the field, how to clean them, and how to cook them.

Cleaning Your Birds

You should clean your birds and cool them as soon as possible, especially in warm weather. This keeps the meat from spoiling.

You'll need the help of an adult to clean your upland bird. Strip the skin with feathers from the breast. Cut out the breast meat on either side of the middle bone of the breast. Now you have meat that is ready for roasting or other cooking methods.

ADULT HELP NEEDED!

Because you'll be using a sharp knife and game shears and working with raw meat, get help from an experienced hunter when cleaning upland game birds.

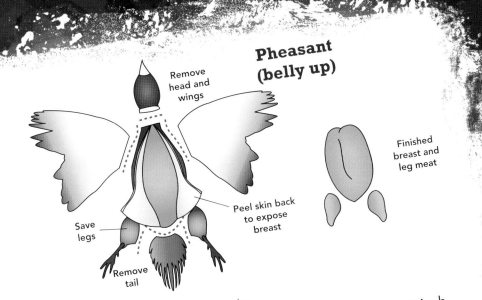

Pheasant (belly up)

Remove head and wings

Peel skin back to expose breast

Save legs

Remove tail

Finished breast and leg meat

Upland Bird Nuggets

Cut the breast and leg meat into strips or chunks about 1 inch (2.5 centimeters) wide. Roll the meat pieces in cornmeal or seasoned flour. Fry or deep-fry the meat in vegetable oil.

Pheasant meat is delicious no matter how you cook it.

GLOSSARY

BAG LIMIT

the maximum number of animals of a species a hunter can kill in a day

CONSERVATION

the thoughtful, efficient, and careful use of natural resources

ETHICS

the way a hunter acts in the field that is fair to the animals and the sport

GAME SHEARS

a sturdy, scissorslike tool designed for cutting game

HABITAT

the place an animal lives, which provides the animal with hiding, food sources, and water

MIGRATE

to move from north to south in the fall and to move from south to north in the spring

NATURAL RESOURCES

things found in nature that are useful for humans

SAFETY

a device on a firearm that keeps it from accidentally firing

SPECIES

animals that are grouped together by scientists because they are related

LERNER e SOURCE

Expand learning beyond the printed book. Download free, complementary educational resources for this book from our website, www.lerneresource.com.

FOR MORE INFORMATION

Further Reading

Landau, Elaine. *Golden Retrievers Are the Best!* Minneapolis: Lerner Publications Company, 2010.

Landau, Elaine. *Labrador Retrievers Are the Best!* Minneapolis: Lerner Publications Company, 2010.

MacRae, Sloan. *Turkey Hunting.* New York: PowerKids Press, 2011.

Websites

Junior Shooters
http://www.juniorshooters.net/
This website features information on hunting clubs, events, and safety geared toward young shooters.

Pheasants Forever
http://www.pheasantsforever.org/
This website is dedicated to hunting pheasants responsibly. It features hunting tips, information about pheasant habitats, and more.

U.S. Fish and Wildlife Service: Hunting
http://www.fws.gov/hunting/
This website has information on conservation, national hunting regulations, and resources on where to go to learn the hunting rules for your own state.

INDEX

About the Author

Tom Carpenter has hunted and fished across North America for almost five decades, pursuing big game, waterfowl, upland birds, wild turkeys, small game, and fish of all kinds. He has raised three sons as sportsmen and written countless articles and contributed to dozens of books on hunting, fishing, nature, and the outdoors.